Table of Contents

Introduction..1
Chapter 1: Introduction to Event Decoration and Styling..5
Chapter 2: Assessing Your Skills and Style........9
Chapter 4: Developing Your Business Plan.....16
Chapter 5: Legal and Regulatory Considerations...20
Chapter 6: Setting Up Your Business Operations..25
Chapter 7: Building Your Brand and Online Presence..30
Chapter 8: Acquiring Clients and Networking. 36
Chapter 9: Providing Exceptional Service........40
Chapter 10: Growing Your Business.................44

Introduction

Welcome to "The Ultimate Guide on How to Start an Event Decoration and Styling Business"! If you've ever dreamed of transforming ordinary spaces into stunning, memorable environments, you're in the right place. This comprehensive guide will walk you through every step you need to take to launch your own successful event decoration and styling business. Let's dive into this exciting journey together and unlock the secrets to creating beautiful, unforgettable events.

Chapter 1: Introduction to Event Decoration and Styling

First things first, let's explore the enchanting world of event decoration and styling. Have you ever wondered what it really means to be an event decorator or stylist? Well, it's all about bringing visions to life, creating atmospheres that captivate, and ensuring every detail contributes to the overall aesthetic. In this chapter, we'll delve into the significance of decoration and styling within the event industry. Whether it's a dream wedding, a sophisticated corporate gala, or a fun-filled private party, you'll discover how impactful and valuable professional event styling can be. We'll also look at the different types of events that benefit from expert styling and how each one presents unique opportunities and challenges.

Chapter 2: Assessing Your Skills and Style

Now, let's turn the spotlight on you. To thrive in the event decoration and styling business, you need a certain set of skills and a distinct sense of style. This chapter is all about self-assessment and discovery. We'll guide you through evaluating your strengths and identifying areas where you might need a bit more practice or training. Additionally, defining your personal style is crucial—it's what sets you apart from the competition. We'll help you understand how your style aligns with what your potential clients are looking for. By the end of this chapter, you'll have a clear picture of your unique stylistic signature and how to leverage it in your business.

Chapter 3: Understanding Your Target Market

Every thriving business is built on a deep understanding of its target market. In Chapter 3, we'll focus on how to identify and analyze your ideal clients. Knowing who they are, what they like, and what they need is key to offering services that resonate with them. We'll dive into demographics, preferences, and trends in the event decoration and styling industry. This insight will help you tailor your services and marketing strategies to attract and retain the right clients for your business.

Chapter 4: Developing Your Business Plan

A well-thought-out business plan is your roadmap to success. In this chapter, we'll walk you through the essential components of crafting a comprehensive business plan for your event decoration and styling venture. You'll learn how to define your business goals and objectives, outline the services you'll offer, and set your pricing strategies. We'll also cover marketing tactics to help you reach your target audience effectively. By the end of this chapter, you'll have a solid plan that will guide you through the initial stages of your business and beyond.

Chapter 5: Legal and Regulatory Considerations

Navigating the legal and regulatory landscape is a crucial part of running a business. In Chapter 5, we'll help you understand the various legal structures available for your business, and what might work best for you. We'll discuss the necessary licenses and permits you'll need, as well as insurance requirements to protect your business and your clients. Ensuring that your business is compliant with all relevant laws and regulations is essential for building a trustworthy and professional reputation.

Chapter 6: Setting Up Your Business Operations

Efficient business operations are the backbone of a successful event decoration and styling business. This chapter will guide you through the practical aspects of setting up your business. From sourcing reliable suppliers and managing your inventory to establishing fair pricing structures and developing clear contracts, we've got you covered. We'll also touch on best practices for streamlining your operations to ensure you can deliver exceptional service to your clients consistently.

Stay tuned for the upcoming chapters where we'll delve into building your brand and online presence, acquiring clients and networking, providing exceptional service, and growing your business. By the end of this guide, you'll have all the knowledge and tools you need to start and thrive in your event decoration and styling business. Let's embark on this exciting journey together and turn your passion into a successful entrepreneurial venture!

Chapter 1: Introduction to Event Decoration and Styling

Event decoration and styling is truly an art form, one that can transform ordinary spaces into stunning, unforgettable experiences. Whether you're planning a wedding, a corporate gala, or a private party, the role of an event decorator and stylist is crucial in creating a visually appealing and cohesive atmosphere that guests will remember. In this chapter, we're going to dive deep into the fascinating world of event decoration and styling. We'll explore why it's so important, the different types of events that benefit from professional styling, and the essential skills you need to excel in this exciting industry.

What is Event Decoration and Styling?

Event decoration and styling involve the creative planning, design, and execution of events to make them visually appealing and captivating. It's about transforming a space into an ambiance that aligns perfectly with the event's theme, purpose, or desired mood. From selecting the right color schemes and decorations to arranging furniture and lighting, event decorators and stylists handle every visual aspect of an event.

One of the main goals of event decoration and styling is to create an immersive and memorable experience for attendees. A well-designed event doesn't just look good—it also feels right, conveying the desired message or atmosphere. Event decorators and stylists work closely with event planners, clients, and other vendors to bring their vision to life and ensure a cohesive and harmonious overall design.

Types of Events That Require Professional Styling

Event decoration and styling are essential for various types of events, including but not limited to:

1. **Weddings**
   Weddings are a prime example of events that require professional decoration and styling. From the ceremony to the reception, every aspect of a wedding can be beautifully curated by an event decorator and stylist. The color palette, floral arrangements, table settings, lighting, and overall ambiance all play significant roles in creating a romantic and magical atmosphere.
2. **Corporate Galas and Events**
   Corporate events, such as galas, conferences, and product launches, often need a sophisticated and professional atmosphere. Event decorators and stylists can transform a plain conference room or ballroom into a stunning space that aligns

with the company's branding and enhances the overall guest experience.

3. **Private Parties and Celebrations**
Whether it's a birthday party, anniversary celebration, or a themed costume party, event decoration and styling can elevate the mood and excitement of any private gathering. From the choice of decorations to the arrangement of furniture and props, event decorators and stylists can create a personalized and immersive experience for both the host and the guests.

Skills Required in Event Decoration and Styling

To succeed in the event decoration and styling industry, several skills are indispensable. These include:

1. **Creativity and Design Eye**
Event decorators and stylists must have a keen eye for design and a creative mindset. They need to be able to envision how various elements will come together to create a visually appealing and cohesive design scheme. Attention to detail and the ability to think outside the box are essential for crafting unique and memorable event experiences.

2. **Strong Communication and Collaboration**
Event decorators and stylists often work closely with clients, event planners, and other vendors. Effective communication

skills are vital to understanding the client's vision, coordinating with different parties, and ensuring the successful execution of the planned design. Collaboration with other professionals in the event industry is key to creating a harmonious and cohesive event.

3. **Organizational and Time-Management Abilities**
   Event decoration and styling involve juggling multiple tasks simultaneously while adhering to strict timelines. Strong organizational skills and the ability to manage time efficiently are critical for managing projects and delivering exceptional results within the given timeframe.
4. **Flexibility and Adaptability**
   Events can be unpredictable, and last-minute changes are not uncommon. Event decorators and stylists must be flexible and adaptable to accommodate changes, solve problems creatively, and ensure the smooth execution of the event.

In the next chapter, we will explore the importance of assessing your skills and defining your personal style in event design and decoration.
Understanding your strengths and preferences will lay the foundation for your success in this industry. Stay tuned for Chapter 2: Assessing Your Skills and Style.

Chapter 2: Assessing Your Skills and Style

To thrive in the event decoration and styling industry, having a solid grasp of your skills and personal style is essential. This chapter is your guide to understanding your abilities, defining your unique style, and leveraging your strengths to build a successful business.

Evaluating Your Skills

Let's start with a self-evaluation of your skills. Event decoration and styling demand a wide range of talents, including creativity, a keen design eye, effective communication, collaboration, organizational abilities, time management, flexibility, and adaptability. Take a moment to assess your proficiency in each of these areas. Where do you excel, and where might you need some improvement?

Reflect on your past experiences in event planning or design-related roles. These can offer valuable insights into your capabilities. Maybe you're great at color coordination, have an exceptional eye for detail, or have a knack for creating unique and visually stunning arrangements. Be honest with yourself during this evaluation process. Acknowledging areas where you need to improve is crucial. Be ready to invest time and effort into developing these skills, whether through courses, workshops, industry events, or seeking mentorship from seasoned professionals.

Defining Your Personal Style

Once you've assessed your skills, it's time to define your personal style in event decoration and styling. Your style is your signature touch, setting you apart from other professionals in the industry. It should reflect your unique perspective and resonate with your target market.

Begin by gathering inspiration from various sources—magazines, online platforms, and attending events. Pay attention to different design elements, color palettes, textures, and themes that inspire you. Look for recurring patterns and themes that align with your personal taste and preferences. Think about the type of events you enjoy styling the most and the atmosphere you want to create. Are you drawn to elegant, romantic weddings, or do you prefer modern, minimalist corporate events? Defining your niche and identifying your preferred style will help you attract the right clients and build a strong brand identity.

Highlighting Your Unique Selling Points

In addition to assessing your skills and defining your personal style, it's essential to pinpoint your unique selling points. What makes you stand out in the event decoration and styling industry? It could be your attention to detail, ability to work within various budgets, or expertise in a specific type of event. Highlighting your unique selling points will help you differentiate yourself from competitors and attract clients who align with your values and vision.

Make sure to communicate these selling points in your marketing materials and when networking with potential clients.

Remember, your skills and style may evolve over time. Regularly reassess and refine them. Continuously seek inspiration, stay updated with current trends, and challenge yourself to grow both personally and professionally. By assessing your skills, defining your personal style, and highlighting your unique selling points, you'll lay a strong foundation for your event decoration and styling business.

In the next chapter, we'll delve deeper into understanding your target market and tailoring your services to meet their specific needs.

Chapter 3: Understanding Your Target Market

Grasping the nuances of your target market is a cornerstone for the success of your event decoration and styling business. By honing in on who your potential clients are and what they truly want, you can tailor your services to perfectly match their needs and preferences. This chapter will walk you through the steps of understanding your target market and positioning your business to attract and serve them with finesse.

Identifying Your Target Market

First things first, let's talk about identifying your target market. This involves looking at a variety of factors such as demographics, psychographics, and behavior. Think of demographics as the basic characteristics of the people or organizations who are most likely to hire you. This includes aspects like age, gender, income level, occupation, and where they live.

For instance, you might find that your typical client is a middle-aged woman planning a high-budget wedding, or perhaps a young professional organizing a corporate event. Each demographic will have different needs and expectations.

But don't stop there. Psychographics are just as crucial. These factors delve into the motivations, values, and lifestyles of your potential clients. Ask yourself about their interests, hobbies, attitudes, and aspirations. Are they environmentally conscious? Do they prefer traditional or modern aesthetics? This kind of information helps you build a richer, more accurate profile of who you should be targeting.

Additionally, understanding your market's behavior is essential. This means analyzing their buying patterns, preferences, and past experiences with event decoration and styling services. Maybe they prefer working with businesses that have a strong online presence, or perhaps they value hands-on customer service above all else. The better you understand these patterns, the more effectively you can tailor your offerings.

Segmenting Your Target Market

Once you've got a handle on who your target market is, it's time to segment it into specific groups. Segmentation allows you to focus your efforts and resources on the most promising segments, making your marketing strategies more efficient and effective.

You can segment your market based on various criteria such as event type, budget, theme, or location. For example, you might decide to specialize in weddings, corporate events, or private parties. Within each segment, consider further categorizing by budget, preferred themes, or specific geographic areas.

By doing this, you can customize your marketing and services to appeal to the unique needs and preferences of each group. This targeted approach not only increases your chances of attracting the right clients but also helps establish you as a specialist in the industry.

Researching Your Target Market

After identifying and segmenting your target market, the next step is conducting thorough research to gain deeper insights. This research is crucial for understanding the needs, preferences, and pain points of your potential clients. Essentially, you want to position your business as the perfect solution to their event decoration and styling challenges.

There are several ways to gather this valuable information. Surveys, interviews, and focus groups are direct methods to get feedback from potential clients. Additionally, studying market trends, industry reports, and competitor analysis can provide a broader view of what your target market is looking for.

Positioning Your Business

With a solid understanding of your target market, you can now position your business to stand out from the competition and attract your ideal clients. This starts with developing a unique selling proposition (USP) that highlights what makes your business different.

Consider focusing on specific event types where you have particular expertise or offering specialized services that cater to niche segments within your target market. For example, you might become known as the go-to event decorator for sustainable, eco-friendly events.

Crafting compelling marketing messages and strong branding that resonate with your target market is key. Showcase your previous work, gather testimonials from satisfied clients, and emphasize your attention to detail and exceptional customer service. These elements build trust and credibility, making it easier for potential clients to choose you over competitors.

Summary

Understanding your target market is vital for the success of your event decoration and styling business. By identifying and analyzing who your potential clients are, segmenting your market, conducting thorough research, and effectively positioning your business, you can attract and serve the right clients. This approach not only differentiates you from competitors but also establishes a strong presence in the industry, ensuring your business thrives.

Chapter 4: Developing Your Business Plan

Creating a comprehensive business plan is like building a solid foundation for your event decoration and styling business. Think of it as your roadmap, guiding you through operations, helping you secure funding, and setting achievable goals for growth and sustainability. Let's dive into how to craft a business plan that will set you up for long-term success.

Why is a Business Plan Important?

A business plan is more than just a document—it's the backbone of your event decoration and styling business. It lays out your vision, mission, and values, while also providing a detailed analysis of the industry, market conditions, and competitors. With a clear plan, you can manage risks more effectively, make informed decisions, and attract potential investors or partners who believe in your vision.

Elements of a Business Plan

1. Executive Summary

Start with an executive summary that encapsulates your business in a nutshell. This section should include your mission statement, target market, competitive advantage, and financial projections. Keep it concise but engaging enough to grab the reader's attention and make them want to learn more about your business.

2. Company Description

In this section, describe your event decoration and styling business in detail. Explain the types of events you specialize in, such as weddings, corporate events, or private parties, and highlight your unique selling points. Discuss the market demand for your services and provide information about your team, location, and any strategic partnerships you have or plan to establish.

3. Market Analysis

Conduct thorough research to gain a deep understanding of the industry, market trends, and customer preferences. Identify your target market segments and assess their needs and preferences. Analyze your competitors to understand their strengths and weaknesses. Use this information to develop marketing strategies that effectively position your business in the market.

4. Marketing and Sales Strategies

Outline your marketing and promotional activities aimed at attracting clients. Describe how you plan to build brand awareness, identify relevant advertising platforms, and establish partnerships or collaborations with other vendors or event professionals. Include a sales strategy that details your pricing structure, packages, and incentives to attract and retain clients.

5. Operations and Management

Detail your day-to-day operational processes and how you plan to manage your event decoration and styling business efficiently. This should include information about your team structure, roles and responsibilities, workflow, and internal communication channels. Develop a timeline for executing events and outline any external resources or vendors you plan to collaborate with.

6. Financial Projections

Create a detailed financial plan that includes projected income and expenses, cash flow forecasts, and a break-even analysis. This section should demonstrate the financial viability and profitability of your business. Consider seeking advice from a financial professional to ensure your projections and financial modeling are accurate.

7. Risk Assessment

Identify potential risks and challenges that may impact your business and develop strategies to mitigate them. This could include having backup vendors, creating contingency plans, or implementing risk management protocols. Being prepared for the unexpected will help you navigate any bumps in the road.

Updating and Revisiting Your Business Plan

Remember, a business plan isn't a static document; it should evolve as your business grows. Regularly review and update your plan, at least annually or whenever significant changes occur in the industry or market conditions. Evaluate your goals, strategies, and financial projections to ensure they align with your current direction and objectives.

Conclusion

In conclusion, developing a comprehensive business plan is essential for the success of your event decoration and styling business. It provides clarity and direction, and serves as a valuable tool for attracting investors, planning your operations, and achieving your growth objectives. Take the time to research, analyze, and craft a well-thought-out plan that sets you up for long-term success. With a solid business plan in place, you'll be well-equipped to turn your creative passion into a thriving business.

Chapter 5: Legal and Regulatory Considerations

Starting an event decoration and styling business is an exciting venture, but it also comes with its fair share of legal and regulatory hurdles. Navigating these requirements can seem daunting, but ensuring your business complies with all relevant laws and regulations is crucial. Doing so not only helps you avoid legal troubles but also protects your brand's reputation. Let's walk through the essential legal and regulatory considerations for starting your event decoration and styling business.

Business Structure

The first step in setting up your business is determining its legal structure. You have several options, including registering as a sole proprietor, forming a partnership, or establishing a limited liability company (LLC). Each structure comes with its own set of advantages and disadvantages. For instance, a sole proprietorship is simple and straightforward but offers little personal liability protection. An LLC, on the other hand, provides liability protection but involves more paperwork and higher costs. It's wise to consult with a legal professional or accountant to choose the most suitable structure for your business based on your specific circumstances.

Business Name and Registration

Choosing a unique and memorable business name is a key part of branding your event decoration and styling business. Before you settle on a name, conduct a thorough search to ensure it's available and not already in use by another company. Once you have your name, you'll need to register it with the appropriate government agency or department. This step helps establish your legal identity and protects your business name from being used by others.

Licenses and Permits

Operating your event decoration and styling business legally often requires obtaining various licenses and permits. The specific requirements can vary depending on your location and the services you offer. Here are some common licenses and permits you might need:

1. **Business License**: This general license is required to legally operate any type of business. Check with your local government for specific requirements and procedures for obtaining this license.
2. **Sales Tax Permit**: If your business involves selling products or tangible items, you may need a sales tax permit to collect and remit sales tax to the appropriate authorities. Research your local sales tax regulations to understand the necessary steps to obtain this permit.

3. **Zoning and Land Use Permits**: Depending on your location, you may need zoning and land use permits to ensure your business activities comply with local regulations. These permits are particularly important if you plan to operate from a physical location or use certain venues for events.
4. **Health and Safety Permits**: If your business involves food preparation or handling, you may need health and safety permits to meet necessary sanitation and hygiene standards. Additionally, if you plan to install temporary structures or stages for events, you may need permits to ensure structural safety.

Insurance

Insurance is a critical component of protecting your event decoration and styling business from unforeseen circumstances. Consider securing the following types of insurance:

1. **General Liability Insurance:** This protects your business from third-party claims for bodily injury, property damage, or personal injury that may occur during events or while providing your services.
2. **Professional Liability Insurance:** Also known as errors and omissions (E&O) insurance, this protects your business if a client alleges you made a mistake or provided negligent services resulting in financial loss.

3. **Property Insurance:** If you own or lease a physical location, property insurance will protect your assets, such as furniture, decorations, and equipment, against damage or theft.
4. **Workers' Compensation Insurance:** If you have employees, workers' compensation insurance covers their medical expenses and lost wages in case of work-related injuries or illnesses.

Consult with an insurance professional to assess your specific needs and determine the appropriate coverage for your event decoration and styling business.

Contracts and Agreements

When working with clients, vendors, or other business partners, it's crucial to establish clear and legally binding contracts and agreements. These documents should outline the scope of services, payment terms, cancellation policies, and any other relevant provisions. Having well-crafted contracts ensures that all parties understand their expectations and responsibilities, protecting your interests and minimizing disputes.

Intellectual Property Protection

As a creative professional, protecting your intellectual property is essential. This can include trademarks, copyrights, or patents for unique designs or concepts. Consult with an intellectual property attorney to determine the best strategies for safeguarding your creative work and preventing others from using it without permission.

Conclusion

Running a legally compliant event decoration and styling business is fundamental to its long-term success. By understanding and fulfilling the legal and regulatory requirements, you can protect your business and build a solid foundation for growth. Make it a priority to consult with professionals in the legal and insurance fields to ensure you adhere to all applicable laws and safeguard your business against potential risks or liabilities. With the right precautions in place, you can focus on creating beautiful, memorable events for your clients.

Chapter 6: Setting Up Your Business Operations

Setting up efficient and organized business operations is crucial for the success and growth of your event decoration and styling business. Think of this as laying the foundation for everything you want to build in the future. In this chapter, we'll walk you through the essential steps to establish and streamline your operations, ensuring you can deliver exceptional service to your clients.

Creating a Business Plan

Before diving into the nitty-gritty of setting up your business operations, it's essential to revisit and refine your business plan. Your business plan acts like a roadmap, outlining your goals, strategies, and financial projections. It's not just a formality—it's a valuable reference that helps you stay focused on your long-term objectives as you navigate the day-to-day operations. Make it a habit to review your business plan regularly and update it as your business evolves. This way, you'll always have a clear direction and be prepared to adapt to any changes.

Financial Considerations

Effective financial management is the backbone of any successful business. Start by determining your startup costs, which include equipment, supplies, marketing, and office space. Create a detailed budget that includes all ongoing expenses such as rent, utilities, insurance, salaries, and marketing. This budget will serve as your financial blueprint, helping you plan and allocate funds appropriately.

Consider hiring an accountant or bookkeeper to assist with financial tasks such as managing invoices, tracking revenue and expenses, and preparing financial reports. If hiring someone isn't feasible at the moment, there are excellent software programs like QuickBooks that can streamline your financial processes and ensure accurate record-keeping. Keeping your finances in order will give you peace of mind and allow you to focus on growing your business.

Inventory and Supplies

In the world of event decoration and styling, having the right supplies on hand is crucial. Start by making a list of the essential items you'll need, such as linens, tableware, centerpieces, drapery, lighting fixtures, and other decorative elements. Research suppliers and wholesalers to find high-quality products at competitive prices. Establish relationships with reliable vendors who can consistently deliver the items you need.

Proper inventory management is crucial to ensure you have everything required for each event. This means keeping track of what you have in stock and knowing when to reorder supplies. An organized inventory system will help you avoid last-minute scrambles and ensure that every event runs smoothly.

Transportation and Logistics

Event decoration and styling often require delivering and setting up decorations at various venues. To do this efficiently, you need a reliable mode of transportation that can accommodate your inventory and equipment. Depending on the size of your business, you might consider purchasing or leasing a van or truck.

Develop a system for logistics and scheduling to ensure smooth coordination of deliveries and setups. Maintain a calendar or scheduling software to track all upcoming events and allocate resources accordingly. Efficient planning and organization will help you meet deadlines and provide exceptional service to your clients.

Workflow and Processes

Establishing streamlined workflows and processes is essential for the efficiency of your business operations. This includes creating a clear system for handling inquiries and bookings, managing client contracts and agreements, and coordinating with vendors and partners. Consider implementing project management software or a customer relationship management (CRM) system to help you track and organize all client interactions and tasks. This will enable you to stay on top of deadlines, communicate effectively with clients and vendors, and ensure a smooth workflow from start to finish.

Team Building and Staffing

As your business grows, you may need to hire additional staff members to assist with event setup, coordination, and administrative tasks. Carefully consider the roles and responsibilities you need to fill and create detailed job descriptions. Recruit and hire individuals who are passionate about event decoration and styling and share your commitment to delivering excellent service. Provide proper training and ongoing support to ensure your team is equipped to meet and exceed client expectations.

Operating Procedures and Quality Control

Developing operating procedures and implementing quality control measures will help ensure consistency and high standards in your event decoration and styling business. Establish guidelines for design processes, setup procedures, and client communication protocols. Regularly evaluate the quality of your work and seek client feedback to continuously improve your services. This will bolster your reputation and attract more clients to your business.

Conclusion

Setting up your business operations effectively is essential for the success of your event decoration and styling business. By creating a solid foundation, implementing efficient workflows, and prioritizing exceptional service, you'll be well on your way to providing memorable and visually stunning experiences for your clients. With a clear plan and the right tools in place, your business will be poised for growth and long-term success.

Chapter 7: Building Your Brand and Online Presence

Building a strong brand and establishing a prominent online presence are vital for the success of your event decoration and styling business. In today's digital age, potential clients often turn to the internet to research and hire professionals for their events. By taking strategic steps to build your brand and online presence, you can attract more clients and stand out from your competition.

Creating Your Brand Identity

Your brand is more than just a logo and color scheme; it's the perception that clients have of your business. It encompasses your values, mission, and unique selling proposition. To create a strong brand identity, follow these steps:

Define Your Values and Mission

Start by identifying the core values and mission of your event decoration and styling business. Your values should reflect the qualities that set you apart from your competitors and resonate with your target market. Your mission statement should communicate your overall purpose and the value you bring to your clients. Think about what drives you and what you want to achieve with your business. This clarity will help you create a brand that truly represents you.

Identify Your Unique Selling Proposition

Determine what makes your business unique and highlight it as your unique selling proposition. This could be your expertise in a specific event type or theme, exceptional attention to detail, custom-design options, or any other aspect that sets you apart. Clearly communicate this unique selling point in your branding materials and online presence. This way, potential clients will understand what makes you the best choice for their event.

Create Consistent Visual Branding

Develop a visually appealing and consistent brand identity that reflects your values and unique selling proposition. This includes choosing a color scheme, typography, and logo design that resonate with your target market and align with your brand identity. Use these visual elements consistently across all your branding materials, including your website, social media profiles, and marketing collateral. Consistency helps build recognition and trust with your audience.

Showcase Your Portfolio

Your portfolio is a powerful tool to showcase your past work and demonstrate your expertise. Include high-quality photos and descriptions of events you have decorated and styled. Organize your portfolio by event type or theme to make it easy for potential clients to navigate and find inspiration. Your portfolio is your chance to shine, so make sure it reflects your best work and unique style.

Establishing Your Online Presence

In addition to creating a strong brand identity, establishing a robust online presence is essential in today's digital age. Here are some steps to help you get started:

Create a Professional Website

Your website will be the cornerstone of your online presence. It should be visually appealing, user-friendly, and provide all the necessary information that potential clients may need. Include an About page that shares your story and showcases your expertise, a Portfolio page to display your work, and a Contact page for inquiries. Consider using professional photography to highlight your work and create a visually stunning website. Your website is often the first impression potential clients will have of your business, so make it count.

Optimize for Search Engines

Ensure that your website is search engine optimized (SEO) so that potential clients can easily find you when searching for event decoration and styling services in your area. Use relevant keywords throughout your website's content, meta descriptions, headers, and image alt tags. Consider creating a blog where you can consistently publish helpful and informative content related to event decoration and styling. SEO is a powerful tool to increase your visibility online.

Utilize Social Media Platforms

Social media platforms such as Instagram, Facebook, Pinterest, and LinkedIn can be powerful tools to showcase your work, engage with potential clients, and build a following. Choose platforms that align with your target market and focus on creating visually appealing and engaging content. Regularly post images and videos of your work, share industry insights, engage with your audience by responding to comments and messages, and collaborate with influencers or other industry professionals. Social media is a great way to connect with a wider audience and showcase your unique style.

Engage with Online Communities

Joining online communities, such as event planning or wedding-related forums and groups, can help you build relationships with potential clients and industry professionals. Actively participate by offering valuable insights, answering questions, and sharing your expertise. This can help establish you as a dependable and knowledgeable professional in the event decoration and styling industry.

Networking is key to growing your business and building your reputation.

Collect and Showcase Testimonials

Testimonials and reviews play a crucial role in building credibility and trust with potential clients. Encourage clients to share their positive experiences and feedback after working with you. Display these testimonials on your website and social media profiles to showcase your exceptional service and client satisfaction. Positive reviews can be a deciding factor for potential clients considering your services.

Continuously Evolve and Adapt

Building your brand and online presence is not a one-time task; it requires continuous efforts and adaptation. Stay updated with the latest trends in both the event decoration and styling industry and the digital marketing landscape. Regularly review and refine your brand identity to ensure it aligns with your target market and differentiates you from your competitors. Actively engage with your online audience and adapt your strategies based on their feedback and preferences. By building a strong brand and establishing an effective online presence, you can attract more clients and position yourself as a top choice in the event decoration and styling industry.

Invest time and effort into creating an appealing brand identity and leveraging online platforms to showcase your work, engage with potential clients, and build credibility. With a compelling brand and online presence, you will be well on your way to growing your event decoration and styling business.

Chapter 8: Acquiring Clients and Networking

When it comes to the event decoration and styling business, finding clients and building a strong network are the keys to success. As you set up your business, you'll need to actively seek out opportunities to connect with potential clients and build relationships with industry professionals. This chapter will walk you through the process of acquiring clients and networking effectively.

Determine Your Ideal Client

Before you jump into marketing and networking strategies, it's essential to identify your ideal client. Think about the types of events you specialize in, your target market segment, and the specific needs and preferences of your clients. By understanding who your ideal client is, you can tailor your marketing efforts to attract and retain them more effectively.

For instance, if you excel in elegant wedding decorations, your ideal client might be brides looking for sophisticated, timeless designs. Alternatively, if you specialize in corporate events, your target might be companies seeking professional and impactful event setups.

Create a Professional Portfolio and Website

A polished and professional portfolio is a must when acquiring clients. Showcase your best work, highlighting different event styles, themes, and designs you've executed. Include high-quality images, detailed descriptions, and glowing testimonials from satisfied clients.

In addition to a portfolio, having a well-designed website is crucial for establishing your online presence. Your website should reflect your brand identity, showcase your portfolio, and provide essential information such as the services you offer, contact details, and pricing. Think of your website as your digital storefront—make it inviting and informative.

Utilize Social Media and Online Platforms

Social media platforms offer a fantastic opportunity to connect with potential clients and showcase your work. Use platforms like Instagram, Facebook, and Pinterest to share images, behind-the-scenes content, event highlights, and to engage with your audience. Regularly update your profiles with fresh content, respond to inquiries and comments, and use relevant hashtags to increase your visibility.

Additionally, consider joining online platforms and directories specifically catered to event planning and decoration. These platforms can help you reach a broader audience and connect with clients who are actively seeking event decoration services.

Attend Networking Events and Workshops

Networking events and industry workshops are excellent for connecting with other professionals in the event industry. Attend industry conferences, trade shows, and local networking events to expand your network and establish meaningful relationships. Be prepared to showcase your work, exchange business cards, and engage in conversations to build connections.

Joining professional associations or organizations related to event planning and decoration is also beneficial. These associations often hold networking events and provide access to exclusive resources and industry insights.

Collaborate with Event Planners and Vendors

Building strong relationships with event planners and other vendors in the industry is crucial for acquiring clients. Event planners often refer clients to trusted decoration and styling professionals, providing a valuable source of leads. Reach out to event planners in your area, introduce yourself and your services, and express your willingness to collaborate.

Additionally, establish relationships with other vendors such as florists, caterers, and rental companies. By partnering with these vendors, you can create a network of professionals who can recommend your services to their clients, thus expanding your client base.

Provide Exceptional Customer Service

Word-of-mouth marketing is incredibly powerful in the event industry, and providing exceptional customer service is key to acquiring and retaining clients. Delight your clients by exceeding their expectations, being responsive to their needs, and delivering outstanding results. Happy clients are more likely to refer you to their friends and colleagues, helping you acquire new clients through positive recommendations.

Conclusion

Acquiring clients and networking in the event decoration and styling business requires a proactive and strategic approach. By identifying your ideal client, showcasing your work through a professional portfolio and website, utilizing social media and online platforms, attending networking events, and collaborating with industry professionals, you can build a strong client base and establish a successful event decoration and styling business. Remember, providing exceptional customer service is key to acquiring and retaining clients in this competitive industry.

Chapter 9: Providing Exceptional Service

Providing exceptional service is the cornerstone of success in the event decoration and styling industry. When clients choose your business, they expect professionalism, meticulous attention to detail, and a smooth, seamless experience. But exceptional service means going beyond just meeting expectations—it's about creating memorable, extraordinary events that leave a lasting impression.

The Importance of Exceptional Service

Why is exceptional service so critical? For starters, it ensures client satisfaction, which is crucial for building a strong reputation and gaining referrals. Happy clients are not only likely to recommend your services to others but also to return for future events. By providing an exceptional experience, you distinguish your business from competitors and establish yourself as a leader in the industry.

Understanding Your Clients

The foundation of exceptional service lies in understanding your clients. This means taking the time to engage in detailed conversations, listening attentively, and asking the right questions. It's important to grasp their vision, budget, timeline, and any specific requirements they may have. The better you understand their needs and preferences, the more effectively you can tailor your services to meet and exceed their expectations.

Effective Communication

Clear and effective communication is essential throughout the event planning process. Keep your clients informed about the progress, updates, and any changes that may arise. Respond promptly to their emails, phone calls, and messages, ensuring they feel valued and heard. Transparency and openness build trust and foster a positive working relationship.

Attention to Detail

Attention to detail is paramount in event decoration and styling. From the initial consultation to the final touches, every element should align with your clients' vision. Be meticulous in your planning and execution, leaving no room for errors or oversights. Striving for perfection in every aspect of your work will help you exceed your clients' expectations and create a flawless event.

Flexibility and Adaptability

Events can be unpredictable, and as an event decorator and stylist, you must be flexible and adaptable. Be prepared for last-minute changes, unexpected circumstances, and unique client requests. Embrace challenges with a positive attitude and find creative solutions to ensure the event runs smoothly, regardless of any hiccups along the way.

Exceptional Customer Service

Exceptional customer service goes beyond delivering a beautiful end result. It's about creating a positive and memorable experience for your clients. Be warm, friendly, and approachable, making them feel comfortable and confident in your abilities. Anticipate their needs, offer solutions, and provide personalized recommendations to enhance their overall experience.

Going the Extra Mile

To truly provide exceptional service, be willing to go the extra mile for your clients. Surprise them with small gestures or added touches that exceed their expectations. Whether it's suggesting a unique centerpiece idea or helping them find the perfect venue, show that you are fully invested in the success of their event. These thoughtful actions can make a significant impact on client satisfaction and loyalty.

Post-Event Follow-Up

The service doesn't end when the event is over. Follow up with your clients to express your gratitude for their trust and support. Send a thank-you note and request feedback on their experience. This not only demonstrates your professionalism but also provides valuable insights for continuous improvement. Showing that you care about their experience even after the event can leave a lasting positive impression.

Conclusion

Providing exceptional service is the bedrock of a successful event decoration and styling business. By understanding your clients, communicating effectively, paying close attention to detail, being flexible, offering outstanding customer service, going the extra mile, and following up after the event, you can ensure that every client's event is a memorable and remarkable experience. This dedication to excellence will not only delight your clients but also help your business thrive in a competitive industry.

So, as you embark on this exciting journey of creating beautiful, unforgettable events, remember that exceptional service is what will set you apart and lead to lasting success.

Chapter 10: Growing Your Business

Growing your event decoration and styling business is a crucial step toward achieving long-term success and sustainability. As your reputation builds and your client base expands, it's essential to have strategies in place to elevate your business to new heights. In this chapter, we'll explore various techniques and considerations for effectively growing your event decoration and styling business.

1. Expanding Services and Offerings

One effective way to grow your business is by broadening the range of services and offerings you provide. Think about diversifying into new event types or adding additional services within your existing niche. For instance, if you primarily focus on weddings, you might consider branching out into corporate events or private parties. Expanding your services not only attracts a wider range of clients but also allows you to cater to the evolving needs and preferences of your current clients.

Conducting market research is key to identifying emerging trends and demands in the event industry. This information will help you tailor your offerings to stay ahead of the curve. For example, if you notice a growing interest in themed corporate events or eco-friendly weddings, you can adjust your services to meet these new demands.

2. Strategic Partnerships

Collaborating with other professionals in the event industry can be a powerful strategy for growing your business. Forming strategic partnerships with event planners, venues, caterers, florists, photographers, and other vendors can help you tap into their networks and gain access to a larger pool of potential clients.

Seek out partnerships that align with your brand values and complement your services. Establishing strong relationships with trusted vendors not only expands your client base but also enhances your reputation as a reliable and well-connected event decoration and styling business. These partnerships can lead to cross-referrals, joint marketing efforts, and a more comprehensive service offering for your clients.

3. Invest in Marketing and Advertising

To grow your business, you need to effectively reach and attract new clients. Investing in marketing and advertising is essential for increasing your brand visibility and generating leads. Here are some marketing avenues to consider:

- **Online Marketing:** Utilize digital channels such as social media platforms, your website, and online advertising to showcase your work, engage with potential clients, and build brand awareness. Implement search engine optimization (SEO) techniques to ensure your business appears prominently in online search results.

- **Print Media:** Explore advertising opportunities in local magazines, newspapers, and event-related publications. Advertising in wedding or event planning guides that are distributed to a targeted audience can be particularly effective.
- **Networking Events:** Attend industry conferences, trade shows, and networking events to connect with potential clients and industry professionals. These platforms are great for showcasing your work, distributing marketing materials, and establishing valuable business contacts.

4. Client Referrals and Testimonials

Word-of-mouth promotion is one of the most powerful tools for growing your event decoration and styling business. Satisfied clients can become your brand advocates, referring your services to their friends, family, and colleagues. Encourage clients to provide testimonials and reviews that highlight their positive experiences working with your business.

Consider implementing a referral program where you offer incentives for clients who refer new business to you. These incentives could be discounts, complementary services, or special perks. By fostering a culture of client referrals, you can build a steady stream of new clients who come to you already primed to appreciate your work.

5. Continuing Education and Skill Development

As the event industry evolves, it's crucial for event decoration and styling professionals to stay updated with the latest trends, techniques, and technologies. Continuing education and skill development not only help you provide exceptional service to your clients but also position your business as a leader in the industry.

Invest in attending workshops, conferences, and training programs that focus on event design, styling, and business management. Staying ahead of the curve allows you to offer innovative solutions to your clients and build a reputation for excellence.

6. Scalability and Operational Efficiency

To successfully grow your business, it's important to ensure that your operations are scalable and efficient. As you take on more clients and expand your service offerings, you need systems and processes in place to handle increased demand.

Consider investing in technology solutions such as project management software, customer relationship management (CRM) tools, and inventory management systems. These tools can help streamline your operations, improve communication with clients and vendors, and enhance overall efficiency. Efficient operations mean you can deliver high-quality services consistently, even as your business grows.

Final Thoughts

Growing your event decoration and styling business requires a strategic approach that focuses on expanding services, building strategic partnerships, investing in marketing efforts, leveraging client referrals, continuing education, and improving operational efficiency. By implementing these growth strategies, you can position your business for long-term success and establish yourself as a trusted and respected professional in the event industry. Embrace the challenges that come with growth and continue to provide exceptional service to your clients, ensuring that every event you touch becomes an unforgettable and extraordinary experience.

www.ingramcontent.com/pod-product-compliance
Lightning Source LLC
Chambersburg PA
CBHW070138230526
45472CB00004B/1582